Rainy Days

by **Trudi Strain Trueit**

Reading Consultant: Nanci R. Vargus, Ed.D.

Marshall Cavendish
Benchmark
New York

Picture Words

 boots

 flowers

 grass

 hats

 pumpkins

 rainbows

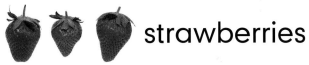 strawberries

 umbrella

 waterfalls

Tip, tap!
Rain hits my .

Rain makes  green.

Rain makes

grow.

Rain makes  bloom.

Rain makes  flow.

Rain makes 🍓🍓🍓 ripe.

Rain makes  glow.

Rain makes wet.

Rain makes wet, too.

Words to Know

bloom
　　to open

flow (floh)
　　to move

glow (gloh)
　　to give off light

ripe
　　fully grown

Find Out More

Books

Herriges, Ann. *Rain*. Minneapolis, MN: Bellwether
Media, 2007.

Jango-Cohen, Judith. *Why Does It Rain?* Minneapolis,
MN: Millbrook Press, 2006.

Kaner, Etta. *Who Likes the Rain?* Toronto, Canada: Kids
Can Press, 2007.

Lakin, Patricia. *Rainy Day!* New York: Dial Books for
Young Readers, 2007.

DVDs

All About Rain, Snow, Sleet, and Hail. Schlessinger
Media, 2000.

All About Wind and Clouds. Schlessinger Media, 2000.

Web Sites

**National Oceanic and Atmospheric Administration
(NOAA): Playtime for Kids**
www.nws.noaa.gov/om/reachout/kidspage.shtml

**University Corporation for Atmospheric Research (UCAR)
Web Weather for Kids: Thunderstorms and Tornadoes**
http://eo.ucar.edu/webweather/thunderhome.html

About the Author

Trudi Strain Trueit loves rainy days, which is a good thing because she was born (and still lives) in the soggy Pacific Northwest. A former television weather forecaster for KAPP TV in Yakima, Washington, and KREM TV in Spokane, Washington, she has written more than forty nonfiction books for kids. Her titles include such topics as rain, snow, hail, and storm chasing. Trudi writes fiction, too, and is the author of the popular *Julep O'Toole* series for middle grade readers. She has a B.A. in broadcast journalism. Learn more about Trudi and her books at **www.truditrueit.com**.

About the Reading Consultant

Nanci R. Vargus, Ed.D., used to teach first grade. Now she works at the University of Indianapolis. Nanci helps young people become teachers. When she moved from California to Indiana, she learned that it can rain year round—even during the summer!

Marshall Cavendish Benchmark
99 White Plains Road
Tarrytown, NY 10591-5502
www.marshallcavendish.us

Library of Congress Cataloging-in-Publication Data
Trueit, Trudi Strain.
Rainy days / by Trudi Strain Trueit
       p. cm. — (Benchmark rebus. Weather watch)
Summary: "Easy to read text with rebuses explores the effects of rain"—Provided by publisher.
Includes bibliographical references.
ISBN 978-0-7614-4012-3
1. Rain and rainfall—Juvenile literature. I. Title.
QC924.7.T7842010
551.57'7—dc22
       2008044239

Editor: Christine Florie
Publisher: Michelle Bisson
Art Director: Anahid Hamparian
Series Designer: Virginia Pope

Photo research by Connie Gardner

Rebus images, with the exception of rainbows, provided courtesy of *Dorling Kindersley*.

Cover photo by: Jim Cummins/Getty Images

The photographs in this book are used by permission and through the courtesy of: *Photo Researchers*: p. 3 Paul G. Adam (rainbow); *Getty Images*: p. 7 Derek Croucher; p. 13 Abi Mar; *Corbis*: p. 5 LWA Dann Tardif; p. 9, 19 Ariel Skelley; p. 11 Roy Morsch; p. 17 Craig Tuttle; p. 21 Ed Bock; *SuperStock*: p. 15 age footstock.

Printed in Malaysia
1 3 5 6 4 2